The Varie
OF CHINA

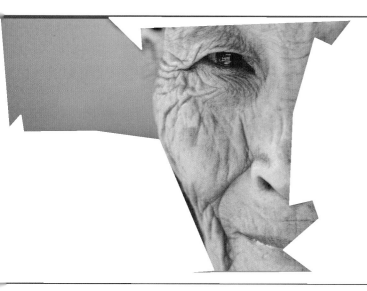

Rob Waring, *Series Editor*

HEINLE
CENGAGE Learning™

Australia • Brazil • Japan • Korea • Mexico • Singapore • Spain • United Kingdom • United States

Words to Know

This story is set in the country of China. It takes place in the remote areas of Yunnan [yunɑn] Province.

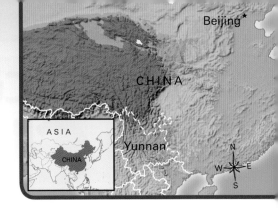

 China's Cultural Diversity. Read the paragraph. Then match each word with the correct definition.

China's mainstream population is mainly Han Chinese, who comprise approximately 90 percent of the country's inhabitants. While the Han are the predominant group, there are also a number of minority nationalities, several of which have unique languages, customs, and mores. With the growing internationalism in China and the world, some fear smaller societies may vanish as cultural lines merge. Brian Schmeck, a documentary filmmaker, wants to record the existence of these charming cultures before they disappear.

1. mainstream _____	**a.** the name of China's biggest ethnic group
2. Han _____	**b.** disappear suddenly
3. mores _____	**c.** pleasing, attractive, delightful
4. vanish _____	**d.** the main or most widely accepted
5. charming _____	**e.** the traditional customs and behaviors of a particular cultural group

B **The Global Village.** Read the paragraph. Then complete the sentences with the correct form of the underlined words or phrases.

For thousands of years, isolation from the world has preserved the traditions of many ethnic and cultural minorities. But now, even the most rural areas of the world are joining the <u>global village</u>. Remote areas may soon have access to <u>satellite</u> TV, cell phones, and other modern technology and will thus no longer be as <u>cut off</u> as they once were. While there are advantages to this modernization, the <u>transition</u> to a more global society may also tempt people to <u>discard</u> their ancient traditions and abandon village life.

1. _____ means to throw something away.
2. A _____ is a change from one condition to another.
3. _____ transmit signals from space to provide information.
4. A location that is _____ is far away from cities and communication.
5. A term for describing a planet without borders or boundaries is _____.

A Mo Suo [mo suo] Woman in Yunnan Province

Outside of China, the culture of the Han Chinese is often considered to be the sole culture of China. While it's true that the population is predominantly Han and over 90 percent of its people are classified as such, China is actually composed of a great number of ethnic minorities. These smaller groups are all quite culturally distinct from the Han Chinese and several have their own languages and customs.

China is presently undergoing extremely high levels of economic development, progress, and rapid change throughout the country. Due to this high level of change and the growth of expansion and development, some feel that it's very important to document the ethnic minorities of the country in some way. Making films about them, for example, would ensure that future generations would be able to gain insights about these cultures, and learn about their languages, beliefs, and mores. One person is committed to recording the way of life of these fascinating people. Brian Schmeck, a documentary filmmaker, has made it his mission to document the vanishing cultures of the 55 minority nationalities of China.

 CD 1, Track 07

Who are these cultural groups and where do they live? According to Schmeck, China's people, also known as 'the fifty-six nationalities of China,' are composed of the Han people and 55 other minority groups. To find these minority nationalities, one must travel to the far edges of China, beyond the great rivers with the deep **gorges**,[1] and across mountains covered in mystery. It is there that one can find a China that has long remained undiscovered and relatively unknown to those who do not live there. Until recently, some foreigners weren't even aware that these aspects of China existed.

In the remoter provinces of the country, such as parts of Yunnan, inhabitants have maintained a way of life with minimal changes over the centuries. These people still use traditional ways of life; some of them still wash their clothes in the river as they have always done, others use oxen to **plow**[2] their land, and work the earth by hand. It's a hard life, but a simpler one as well, with a close sense of family and a powerful work ethic. It is also a way of living that may be in danger of being discarded for the fast and easy way of progress.

---

[1]**gorge:** a high, narrow opening between mountains, usually with a stream or river
[2]**plow:** use a farm implement (a plow) to turn over earth for planting crops

As one watches one of the ethnic groups wearing traditional dress and doing a cultural dance, it becomes apparent that they are quite dissimilar from the high-fashion city residents on the streets of Beijing and Shanghai. In appearance and language, some cultures are distinctly different from those of mainstream China; however, the distinction doesn't end there. The groups vary not only in the way they look and the languages they speak, but also in the arts, such as in the songs and dances of their culture. In fact, these discrete groups differ in many aspects of their culture and stand out as being individual and unique.

For thousands of years, isolation from the world has preserved the traditions of China's ethnic and cultural minorities. Now, however, things are changing. Even the most rural areas of the country are joining the global village. Some of the most remote homes now have access to TV, phones, and the Internet through satellite connections. This in turn means that often for the first time in their history, they can have regular contact with the rest of the world and continual access to what is happening elsewhere. These previously isolated groups are no longer as cut off, and the results of the change are interesting.

Schmeck's experience suggests that the people in these ethnic minorities are not upset by what they see on their TV screens. In fact, it seems extremely attractive and appealing to them. Schmeck explains, "I mean, they see the outside world that they've never seen before and they like what they see." In fact, many of the villagers like it so much that they don't want to sit by passively and watch it. They want to join it.

For a year and a half, filmmaker Brian Schmeck has been traveling across China, rushing to complete a video **archive**[3] of its minority cultures. Why the hurry? Schmeck explains that he feels these peoples' ways of living are rapidly changing, and for him it's important to record it before their ways of the past vanish completely. He believes that he may become one of the last witnesses to some of the traditions of these cultures.

After enjoying a dance with one of the local ethnic groups, Schmeck comments about his mission: "Ten to fifteen years from now," he says, "you're not going to see what I'm seeing. People themselves will still exist, but their ideas, their culture, their way of life will not. It'll be gone, and it's disappearing really fast." The films that Schmeck is making are intended to record the amazing cultural diversity of the 55 minority nationalities of China, both for himself and for **posterity**.[4]

---

[3] **archive:** a collection of historical interest
[4] **posterity:** future generations of people alive after one's death

The Mo Suo people of Yunnan Province are just one example of the 55 minority nationalities. The cultural mores of this fascinating people differ rather significantly from the rest of the world. For example, they have a matriarchal society while most of the rest of the world consists of patriarchal societies, where the opposite gender plays the lead role. Interestingly enough, the Mo Suo language has no word for 'marriage,' since the concept doesn't exist in their culture in a way that most of the world understands.

On one of his journeys to the rural areas of China, Schmeck visits the home of the Mo Suo. To get there, he must cross a large lake and relies on local help, in this case, a very friendly elderly woman. As the woman of nearly 70 rows Schmeck and his crew across the large body of water, she sings cheerfully in the language of the Mo Suo people.

Less than a decade ago, this area of Yunnan was rarely visited by outsiders, but now city residents like a young woman named **Mei Zhou**[5] come here as tourists. Mei explains that spending time in these remote regions gives urban Chinese a chance to enjoy nature. She adds that many find the local inhabitants interesting and the charming villages are often a welcome break from all the activity of the big city. As one enjoys the beautiful scenery surrounding the lake, it's interesting to consider that as a result of people's rising interest in minority cultures and the Mo Suo people, a 67-year-old grandmother can now earn a living in the tourist industry and she truly seems to enjoy her work.

---

[5]**Mei Zhou:** [meɪ joʊ]

Infer Meaning

1. What does the word 'matriarchal' mean? Look at the words around it and write a definition.

2. What does the word 'patriarchal' mean? Look at the words around it and write a definition.

The **Naxi**[6] people, who live in the northwestern part of Yunnan Province, are another example of the cultures of the 55 minority nationalities. They have lived in a charming mountain village for at least 1,500 years. For most of that time, they've been largely cut off from other people, mainly because no road came anywhere near the village.

The lack of a road has created an enormous challenge for the Naxi. No road means no transport; and no transport means that its citizens are forced to walk everywhere. However, these days, things are changing. A village leader says that children now have to walk only two hours to get to a new road to catch a bus to school. Though two hours may seem a lot to most of us, it's a considerable improvement in this isolated region of the world.

While the opportunity to receive an education is an excellent chance for the children of this remote area, the village leader is concerned. He worries that after they receive an education, the young people may see no reason to come back to this little village with its donkey tracks and its simple lifestyle. He anticipates that most of them will want to move to the big city, which could eventually mean the end of this small village.

---

[6]**Naxi:** [nɑʃi]

It appears that the fears of the leaders of the Naxi village may just come true. People throughout rural China are flooding into large cities like **Chongqing**,[7] searching for things they know exist because they've seen them on TV or heard about them from others. The problem is that they can't get these things out in the country. What they are looking for is something that is totally understandable for most. These young people are heading to the bigger cities mainly in search of material possessions and a better life. Brian Schmeck explains: "Modern conveniences, I mean nice housing. They like this and they want to go this way, so in a sense they're getting a better life, but they're forgetting where they came from."

---

[7] **Chongqing:** [tʃɔŋtʃɪŋ]

As Schmeck says, it's easy for people to forget the culture of their village once they become established in the city. For many of the 55 minority nationalities of China, there seems to be a rush to conform to the rest of the country, and that's not necessarily a good thing if you believe that diversity is important. "They're going to be absorbed into mainstream China," says Schmeck, adding that the rich cultural traditions of the ethnic minorities could someday become nothing more than a tourist attraction. "You're going to see it in a dinner theater or a floor show," he says. "Or you're going to go up to a tourist park and **a bunch of**[8] people will be putting on costumes to give you a little display of what was there." Once cultures get to this point, of course, they often become something to look at, like pictures in a museum, rather than a real living piece of history and tradition.

Increasingly, China and the rest of the world are facing greater change and globalization. To think minority cultures here and around the world can be **immune**[9] to that transition is obviously unrealistic. As China charts its course through the early part of the 21st century and continues its high-speed economic development, an emphasis on preserving traditional culture will be increasingly important. It's important that the people of China's 55 minority nationalities do not give up their cultural heritage and that they don't completely discard their ancient traditions for a new way of life. The varied cultures of China must be encouraged to preserve their history because it's their diversity that so greatly **enriches**[10] our world.

---

[8]**a bunch of:** *(slang)* a lot of
[9]**immune:** unaffect⋯ something
[10]**enri⋯** ⋯ mo⋯ ⋯asing

Fact or Opinion?

Look at the following statements. Write 'F' for those that are factual, or 'O' for those that are an opinion.

1. The rush to conform is not a good thing if one believes diversity is important. _____

2. The minority cultures of China will definitely be absorbed in the mainstream. _____

3. China is quickly developing economically. _____

4. Minority cultures will become extinct. _____

After You Read

1. On page 4, filmmaking is given as an example of what?
   A. China's economic development
   B. a way to document something for history
   C. the rapid changes happening in China
   D. how to teach rural people about progress

2. Where does the writer say the 55 minority nationalities of China are located?
   A. in the Yunnan province
   B. near China's great rivers
   C. in remote regions of the country
   D. No one knows.

3. The word 'inhabitant' in paragraph 2 on page 7 is closest in meaning to:
   A. participant
   B. unified
   C. compile
   D. resident

4. Some of China's ethnic and cultural minority nationalities are different from the Han nationality in all of the following ways EXCEPT:
   A. nationality
   B. attraction to modernism
   C. language
   D. cultural ways

5. What is 'it' referring to in the last line of page 8?
   A. television
   B. the outside world
   C. a minority group
   D. isolation

6. What does Brian Schmeck claim on page 11?
   A. National erosion is going to affect the local ethnic groups.
   B. He is the only foreigner to see these ethnic minorities.
   C. He doesn't have enough time to film every minority.
   D. Within 15 years many of these cultures will be gone.

7. The Mo Suo language has no word for _____.
   A. marriage
   B. matriarch
   C. patriarch
   D. gender

8. Which of the following is a suitable heading for the last paragraph on page 12?
   A. Grandmother Rows Boat
   B. Tourism Affects Region
   C. Urban Residents Come Seeking Activity
   D. Tourists Work in Villages

9. What does the word 'anticipate' mean in paragraph 3 on page 15?
   A. contrast
   B. change dramatically
   C. expect
   D. be forthcoming

10. What concern is expressed by the Naxi village leader on page 15?
   A. His village will eventually be abandoned.
   B. Students have to walk two hours to get to a bus.
   C. Lack of transport is hurting the village.
   D. Village children don't get a good enough education.

11. The young people of Naxi village are used as an example of:
   A. those who must document the past
   B. a group not compatible with contemporary China
   C. people transitioning to a new way of life
   D. an ongoing trend in China's 55 minority nationalities

12. Which of the statements best expresses the writer's opinion on page 18?
   A. Ethnic minorities are a valuable part of world culture.
   B. The modern world is going to destroy all villages.
   C. Schmeck can help stop China's economic development.
   D. Tourist parks are a useful way to preserve traditions.

Times

THE WORLD HERITAGE ORGANIZATION: PRESERVING OUR PAST

Today many organizations, both local and global, are devoted to preserving works of art, buildings, and even entire cities. The World Heritage Organization (WHO) is one such group. The following is a brief update on what is being done to preserve cultural heritage worldwide.

The Tombs of Buganda Kings in Kampala, Uganda

The Buganda are one of eight tribal groups who have lived in Uganda for centuries. By 1750 they had created a well-planned centralized form of government. Their leader, called the Kabaka, was assisted by a prime minister as well as the head of the army and the commander of the navy. Over the years, the tribe has continued to maintain many of their original customs and beliefs. Tribal loyalty

The Burial Site of the Bugandan Kings of Kampala

WHO Heritage Sites

Continent	Specific Location	Type of Site	Current Status
Africa	Kampala, Uganda	burial site of several kings	declared a WHO site in 2001
South America	Quito, Ecuador	historic city established in 1500s	declared a WHO site in 1978
Europe	Scotland, U.K.	ancient wall built by the Romans	declared a WHO site in 2008

remains important to the Bugandans, even as many of them leave the country to make lives for themselves overseas. In 1884, in order to preserve and honor the memory of the former kings, the palace grounds of the Kabaka were turned into a burial ground for them. In 2001, WHO declared the area an official World Heritage Site.

The City of Quito, Ecuador

Before Europeans arrived in 1532, Ecuador was part of the great Inca kingdom. The area that is now called Quito became an important political center, and by the end of the 1500s the main streets of the city had been laid out and remain essentially the same today. As part of Quito's early development, many grand public buildings such as palaces and cathedrals were constructed and decorated with beautiful statues and paintings. A powerfully original form of artwork emerged, combining European and South American Indian influences. This style of art greatly influenced the development of art in Latin America over the next 200 years and resulted in Quito being declared a WHO site in 1978.

The Antonine Wall in Scotland, United Kingdom

The Antonine Wall is a 37-mile-long earth and stone barrier built across Scotland by the Romans to protect its lands to the south from invasion by enemy groups. It was begun in A.D. 140 and completed two years later. Originally, forts were built every six miles along the wall, but this was later increased to every two miles. Today, the remains of the wall are clearly visible in many areas along its length, and it just recently became an official WHO site.

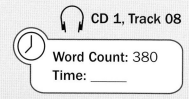

CD 1, Track 08

Word Count: 380

Time: _____

Vocabulary List

archive (11)
a bunch of (18)
charming (2, 12, 15)
cut off (3, 8, 15)
discard (3, 7, 18)
enrich (18)
global village (3, 8)
gorge (7)
immune (18)
mainstream (2, 8, 18, 19)
mores (2, 4, 12)
plow (7)
posterity (11)
satellite (3, 8)
transition (3, 18)
vanish (2, 4, 11)